SEXUAL VIOLENCE AND HARASSMENT

Dealing with Dating and Romance

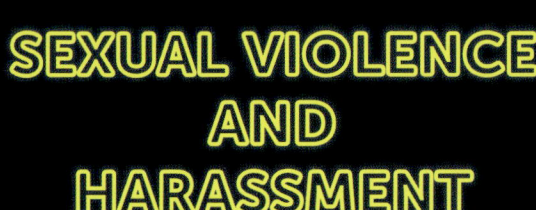

SEXUAL VIOLENCE AND HARASSMENT

ABUSE AMONG FAMILY AND FRIENDS

COPING WITH SEXUAL VIOLENCE AND HARASSMENT

DEALING WITH DATING AND ROMANCE

PREVENTING SEXUAL ASSAULT AND HARASSMENT

SEXUAL VIOLENCE AND HARASSMENT

Dealing with Dating and Romance

Mason Crest
450 Parkway Drive, Suite D
Broomall, Pennsylvania 19008
(866) MCP-BOOK (toll-free)
www.masoncrest.com

Copyright © 2020 by Mason Crest, an imprint of National Highlights, Inc. All rights reserved. No part of this publication may be reproduced or transmitted in any form or by any means, electronic or mechanical, including photocopying, recording, taping, or any information storage and retrieval system, without permission from the publisher.

First printing
9 8 7 6 5 4 3 2 1

ISBN (hardback) 978-1-4222-4202-5
ISBN (series) 978-1-4222-4199-8
ISBN (ebook) 978-1-4222-7608-2
Cataloging-in-Publication Data on file with the Library of Congress.

Developed and Produced by National Highlights Inc.
Editor: Peter Jaskowiak
Interior and cover design: Annemarie Redmond
Production: Michelle Luke

QR CODES AND LINKS TO THIRD-PARTY CONTENT
You may gain access to certain third-party content ("Third-Party Sites") by scanning and using the QR Codes that appear in this publication (the "QR Codes"). We do not operate or control in any respect any information, products, or services on such Third-Party Sites linked to by us via the QR Codes included in this publication, and we assume no responsibility for any materials you may access using the QR Codes. Your use of the QR Codes may be subject to terms, limitations, or restrictions set forth in the applicable terms of use or otherwise established by the owners of the Third-Party Sites. Our linking to such Third-Party Sites via the QR Codes does not imply an endorsement or sponsorship of such Third-Party Sites or the information, products, or services

TABLE OF CONTENTS

Series Introduction 6
Introduction 8
Chapter 1: Teen Dating Violence 11
Chapter 2: The Dynamics of Abuse 29
Chapter 3: What Do I Do Now? 47
Chapter 4: Building Healthy Relationships 57
Series Glossary of Key Terms. 72
Further Reading & Internet Resources. 74
Index 76
Author's Biography & Photo Credits 80

KEY ICONS TO LOOK FOR:

Words to Understand: These words with their easy-to-understand definitions will increase the reader's understanding of the text, while building vocabulary skills.

Sidebars: This boxed material within the main text allows readers to build knowledge, gain insights, explore possibilities, and broaden their perspectives by weaving together additional information to provide realistic and holistic perspectives.

Educational Videos: Readers can view videos by scanning our QR codes, providing them with additional educational content to supplement the text. Examples include news coverage, moments in history, speeches, iconic sports moments, and much more!

Text-Dependent Questions: These questions send the reader back to the text for more careful attention to the evidence presented there.

Research Projects: Readers are pointed toward areas of further inquiry connected to each chapter. Suggestions are provided for projects that encourage deeper research and analysis.

Series Glossary of Key Terms: This back-of-the-book glossary contains terminology used throughout the series. Words found here increase the reader's ability to read and comprehend higher-level books and articles in this field.

DEALING WITH DATING AND ROMANCE

SERIES INTRODUCTION

You may have heard the statistics. One in 4 girls and 1 in 6 boys are sexually abused before turning 18 years old. About 20 percent of American women are raped at some point in their lives. An online survey in 2018 found that approximately 81 percent of women have experienced some form of harassment.

Crimes like these have been happening for a very long time, but stigma surrounding these issues has largely kept them in the shadows. Recent events such as the Me Too movement, the criminal prosecutions of men like Bill Cosby and Dr. Larry Nassar, and the controversy surrounding the confirmation of Judge Brett Kavanaugh to the U.S. Supreme Court have brought media attention to sexual violence and harassment. As it often happens, increased media attention to a social problem is excellent in many ways — the availability of information can help people avoid being victimized, while also letting survivors know that they are not alone. Unfortunately, the media spotlight sometimes shines more heat than light, leaving us with even more questions than we had when we started.

> Teen Dating Violence Hotline
> 1-866-331-9474
> TTY: 1-866-331-8453
> En Español: 1–800–799–7233
> Text: "loveis" to 22522

That is particularly true for young people, who are just dipping their toes into the proverbial dating pool and taking their first steps into the workplace. Two volumes in this set (*Preventing Sexual Assault and Harassment* and *Coping with Sexual*

SERIES INTRODUCTION

Assault and Harassment) address the "before" and "after" of those very difficult situations. The volume *Dealing with Dating* looks at romance – how to date as safely as

> National Sexual Assault Hotline
> 1-800-656-HOPE (4673)
> Online chat: https://www.rainn.org

possible, how to build emotionally healthy relationships, and what to do if something goes wrong. And finally, *Abuse among Family and Friends* takes a look at the painful issue of sexual abuse and exploitation of minors – the vast majority of whom are abused not by strangers, but by family members, acquaintances, and authority figures who are already in the young person's life. These books hope to provide a trustworthy, accessible resource for readers who have questions they might hesitate to ask in person. *What is consent really about, anyway? What do I do if I have been assaulted? How do I go on a date and not be scared? Will my past sexual abuse ruin my future relationships?* And much more.

In addition to the text, a key part of these books is the regularly appearing "Fact Check" sidebar. Each of these special features takes on common myths and misconceptions and provides the real story. Meanwhile, "Find Out More" boxes and dynamic video links are scattered throughout the book. They, along with the "Further Reading" pages at the end, encourage readers to reach out beyond the confines of these pages. There are extraordinary counselors, activists, and hotline operators all over North America who are eager to help young people with their questions and concerns. What to do about sexual violence and harassment is a vital but difficult conversation; these books aspire to be the beginning of that discussion, not the end.

DEALING WITH DATING AND ROMANCE

INTRODUCTION

What is dating, anyway? In the past, a "date" tended to be a pretty specific type of event. A boy arrived at a girl's house, awkwardly greeted her parents, then took her to the movies or dinner. That still happens, of course, but dating doesn't necessarily look like that anymore.

The word *dating* means different things to different people. Sometimes kids in middle school say they are "going out," though they don't actually go anywhere. Often, they text each other a lot, or eat lunch at the same table. For teens, "dating" may involve a lot of hanging out together with a larger social group. These days, of course, dating can involve people of the opposite sex or the same sex. People can also date more than one person at a time, and in "poly" relationships, a group of people may date one another. And then there's "hookup culture" — casual encounters with people who may be friends but may not even be that.

Perhaps surprisingly, our ideas about how abuse can happen in relationships haven't kept up with the evolving nature of relationships themselves. If you were to picture an "abusive relationship," you might immediately think of a straight man hitting a straight woman. That's not wrong, but it's too limited — in truth, anyone can potentially commit abuse. Not all abusers fit the stereotype, either in terms of gender or sexual preference. In a survey quoted by the Centers for Disease Control and Prevention (CDC), roughly 1 in 10 high school students had experienced physical and/or sexual abuse by someone they dated within the previous

INTRODUCTION

year. Notice that the statistic refers to *students*, not just young women. Although straight men are stereotyped as being "the abusers" (and certainly that is often true), it's also true that they also can be the victims of dating abuse.

It's also important to know that abuse comes in many forms that don't involve violence, such as emotional, sexual, or digital abuse. Stalking is also a very dangerous type of abuse that can take place between people who are, or once were, dating.

Whatever shape your dating life takes, there is always the potential for abuse. Abuse has profound and damaging impacts, but that doesn't mean the marks are always visible. It's important to know the warning signs and how to keep yourself safe.

FACTS ON DATING ABUSE

The National Domestic Violence Hotline sponsored a special project on teen dating abuse called Love is Respect (www.loveisrespect.org). The site provides some fascinating – and disturbing – statistics on the issue of teen dating violence.

- Among high school students, 1 in 10 has been hit or slapped by a partner.
- Among college women, 43 percent have experienced some form of abuse from someone they were dating, and 16 percent had been sexually abused.
- Females between 16 and 24 years old are the most common victims of abuse: the rate is about three times higher than any other demographic group.
- Among the teens who have experienced teen dating violence, about two thirds (77 percent) never told anyone about the problem.

DEALING WITH DATING AND ROMANCE

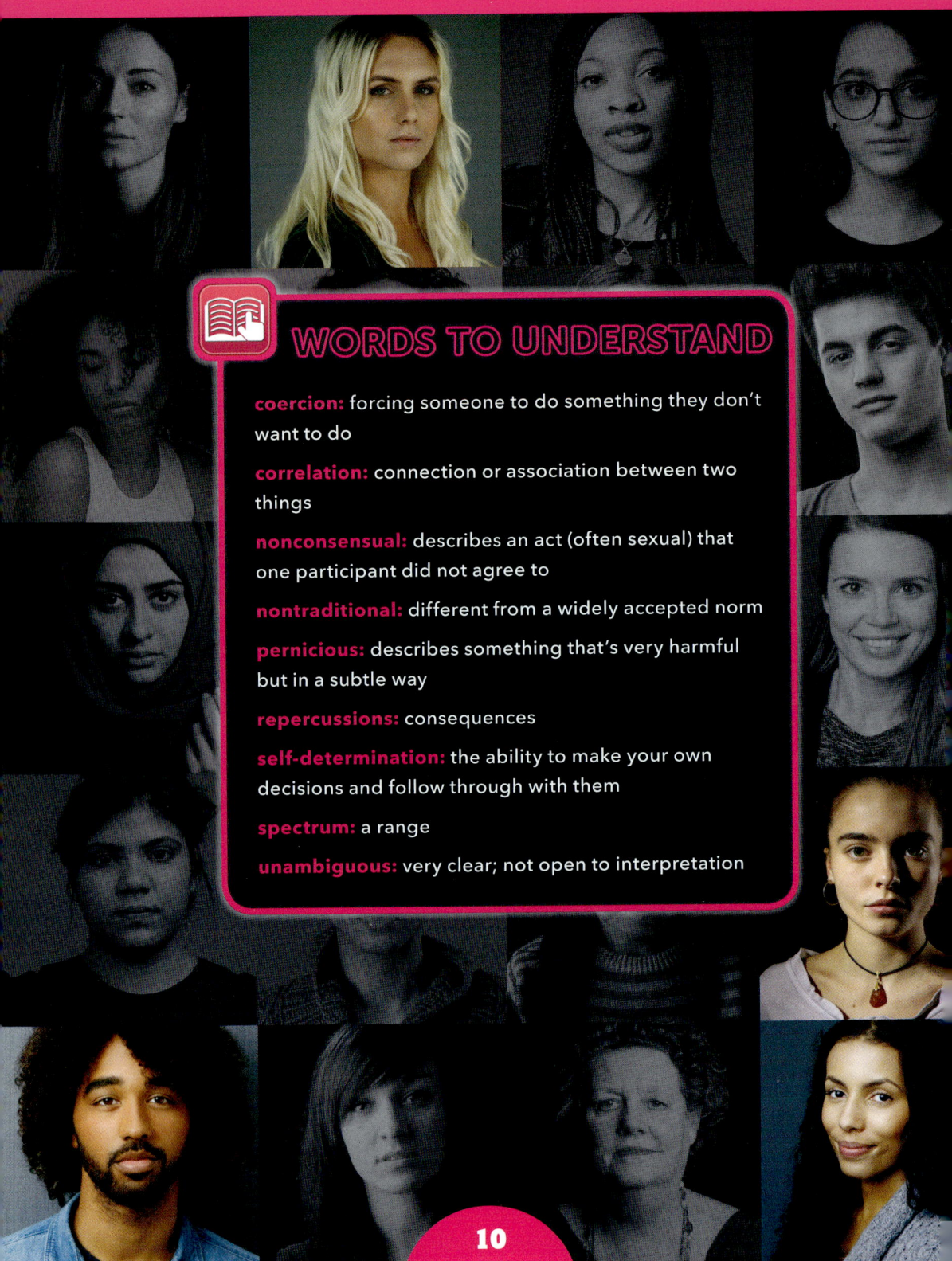

WORDS TO UNDERSTAND

coercion: forcing someone to do something they don't want to do

correlation: connection or association between two things

nonconsensual: describes an act (often sexual) that one participant did not agree to

nontraditional: different from a widely accepted norm

pernicious: describes something that's very harmful but in a subtle way

repercussions: consequences

self-determination: the ability to make your own decisions and follow through with them

spectrum: a range

unambiguous: very clear; not open to interpretation

CHAPTER 1

TEEN DATING VIOLENCE

Too often, young people are mistreated in their relationships, but they tell themselves it "doesn't count" because the relationship is casual or **nontraditional**. That's not true – it counts. If you're a young man, you might be telling yourself that you can't be abused because you're physically stronger than your partner. That's not true, either – men can also be abused.

If you are in *any type* of dating relationship with another person, whether there's sex involved or not, and that person.

- frequently insults you,
- constantly criticizes you,
- tries to control what you do,
- stalks you,
- threatens you,
- physically hurts you, and/or
- tries to force you into sexual activity,

that is abuse. For the purposes of this book, we'll call it *teen dating violence*. It is not okay, not ever. It counts. This chapter will discuss the different types of abuse that can occur and who is affected by them.

WHAT IS TEEN DATING VIOLENCE?

You might have heard the terms *domestic violence* or *intimate partner violence* and concluded that these terms can't apply to your relationship because you aren't married or living together. You might not even consider your relationship to be particularly serious. On the other hand, maybe it *is* serious, but you haven't been sexually intimate yet. Or maybe you are dating someone of the same gender, and you think that abuse is something only straight men do to straight women.

That's why experts have started to prefer to the term *teen dating violence*. It's an umbrella term for a whole **spectrum** of abusive behaviors, ranging from rape to physical assault all the way to seemingly "minor" things like insults and humiliation. It's better to think of teen dating violence as a pattern of behavior over time, rather than one isolated incident.

The term *teen dating violence* is considered an improvement on earlier names, but it's not perfect. The word *violence* may make you think that someone has to be hit to be abused. In reality, not all abusive behaviors include physical violence.

WARNING SIGNS OF ABUSE

- Frequent/intense jealousy
- Demeaning your accomplishments
- Controlling who you see or how you spend time
- Breaking things that belong to you
- Insulting/criticizing you
- Pressuring you for sex or to use alcohol or drugs
- Intimidating, threatening, or scaring you

TEEN DATING VIOLENCE

A NOTE ON TERMS

Throughout this book, the word *partner* is used to refer to any person you're currently dating, thinking about dating, or have dated in the past. The gender of that person doesn't matter, nor does the level of seriousness of your relationship. Here, "partner" might mean someone you're only seeing casually, or even someone you just met! The term was chosen to avoid having to say "boyfriend" or "girlfriend" or "ex" over and over. "Partner" doesn't require that you have to consider the person to be a "life partner" in the committed way that people in long-term relationships do. That's okay, the advice here still applies!

THE SCOPE OF THE PROBLEM

In one study, the American Psychological Association concluded that 1 in 3 teens had experienced some form of abuse in their romantic relationships, whether physical, sexual, verbal, or emotional. Most commonly, males are the perpetrators, but that's not always the case. Both genders can commit teen dating violence, and both genders can be victims of it. According to the CDC, 11 percent of teenage boys experience some form of abusive behavior. For girls, that number is even higher — one study reported that 25 percent of teenage girls had at some point experienced abusive behavior from someone they were dating. The Youth Behavior Risk Survey, on the other hand, found that 1 out of 8 girls and 1 out of 13 boys had experienced physical violence on a date at some point in the 12 months before the survey was taken. In another survey, 54 percent of high school students reported knowing someone in their peer group who'd been abused.

Unfortunately, the news gets worse. More than half of the women who are murdered die at the hands of their partner or ex — and yes, that *includes* teen girls. On average, 2.5 women and teen girls die at the hands of an intimate partner or ex every single day. In most cases, the killings don't come out of nowhere; they are the culmination of a long-standing pattern of abusive behavior.

More broadly, teen dating violence has been directly connected to a number of mass shootings. The 2018 shootings at Great Mills High School in Lexington Park, Maryland, at Marjory Stoneman Douglas School in Parkland, Florida, and at Santa Fe High School, outside Houston, Texas, can all be connected back to abusive dating behavior on the part of the killers. Ex-girlfriends were primary targets in two of the crimes, while a young woman who had turned down the killer's advances was a primary target in

TEEN DATING VIOLENCE

MASS SHOOTINGS AND ABUSE

There is a strong **correlation** between mass shooting events and intimate partner violence. One study found that 54 percent of shootings with four or more victims can be directly connected to family violence.

A memorial for the 17 victims of the 2018 shooting at Marjory Stoneman Douglas High School, in Parkland, Florida.

the third case. Consequently, it's clear that teen dating violence isn't just a problem for the immediate victims — it can be a question of life-or-death for an entire community.

PHYSICAL ABUSE

Physical violence toward another person is sometimes called *assault and battery* or just *battery*. To understand why, it's worth taking a moment to look at a few legal definitions, because the terminology can get a little confusing.

In legal terms, if you commit *assault*, that means you took an action that made another person reasonably believe you might hurt them. The offense of assault is about the threat of violence, not the violence itself — it's a choice (or action) that creates a reasonable fear of harm. *Battery*, on the other hand, is the legal term for actual violence — the act of physically hurting someone. A person can technically be guilty of assault (for instance, raising a fist) but innocent of battery (when the fist connects with another person). Alas, the first frequently leads to the second, which is why you'll hear *assault and battery* used as one phrase.

Hitting, scratching, kicking, and biting are all types of battery. So is grabbing someone — whether by the hair or any other part of the body. Physically stopping someone from leaving a room is also battery, whereas standing in front of a door to threaten someone who tries to leave would be assault. And of course anything involving pointing a weapon (gun, knife, or other) at another person is, at minimum, an assault.

By one estimate, intimate partner violence costs the United States approximately $37 billion per year. That includes the costs of medical treatments, police investigations, lawyers and court costs, counseling, and lost productivity at work. According to the CDC, more than 10 million Americans are subjected to physical violence by their partners every year. That includes both women and men, and it works out to 20 people battered *every minute*.

SEXUAL ASSAULT AND ABUSE

Rape, which may be called *sexual assault* depending on the laws in your state, is the crime of forcing another person into unwanted sexual activity. It's important to understand that the activity might be forced intercourse, but it doesn't have to be: forced oral sex is also a form of rape. Another form is *statutory rape*, which is sex with someone who is too young to give legal consent (even if they think they can). Having sex with someone who is very intoxicated can also be rape, if the person is found to be incapable of consenting to what was happening.

The existence of a long-term relationship does not mean that someone can't be raped by their partner. It doesn't matter whether you said wedding vows, moved in together, or just agreed to "go steady" — *none of that* erases your right to consent or not consent to sexual activity.

OTHER TYPES OF SEXUAL ABUSE

Sexual assault is far from the only type of abuse that can occur. Unwanted touching or kissing is also abusive. Sometimes people have a tendency to excuse "minor" behavior like that — they say, "Well, it wasn't rape, so it wasn't *that* bad." But all sexual abuse is bad.

One type of abusive behavior that many teens experience is pressure to "do more" sexually than they are ready for. Your partner might push for more sexual activity because he or she has more experience than you, or because he or she has different expectations

FACT CHECK!

Myth: *If someone doesn't actively resist sexual intercourse ("fight back"), then it's not assault.*

Fact: Sexual activity needs active consent; "she didn't say no" is not a defense against a rape charge.

DEALING WITH DATING AND ROMANCE

It's abusive to make your partner feel like she "owes" you sex because of something nice you did for her.

about how much sexual activity is "normal." Now, is pressuring or guilting someone into sex "as bad" as physically forcing them to do it? No, obviously it's not "as bad." But that doesn't make it okay. Nor is the related type of pressure, in the form of demanding that you share sexually explicit images or texts. (See page 25 for more on the practice of sexting **coercion**.)

If you find yourself in this situation, remember that your body belongs to you and nobody else. No one gets to decide what you do, "how far" you go, or what body parts you let someone see. Only you know what is right for you — not the media, not your friends, and not even your partner. Any partner who is worthy of you will not push you to do things you're not ready for.

Another type of sexually abusive behavior is preventing someone from using contraception. A man who either refuses to wear a condom when asked or says he will but then takes it off partway through is being abusive. (The nickname for this is "stealthing"; see page 19 for more info.) Likewise, engaging in "rough sex play" can also be abusive if everyone involved has not given clear and **unambiguous** consent, or if someone asks to stop but is ignored.

TEEN DATING VIOLENCE

WHAT IS STEALTHING?

Stealthing is slang for removing a condom during sex after having promised you'd use one. Stealthing violates a partner's trust, and it imposes one person's will over the wishes of the other. If you're stealthing, you're lying – you said you would, then you deliberately didn't. There's no doubt that stealthing is abusive. But is it illegal?

In the United States, the best answer we can give is a vague, "not exactly, but…." Currently, no specific criminal statute forbids stealthing. That said, if a man is aware that he has a sexually transmitted disease (STD), and he removes the condom anyway, that is illegal and could even rise to the level of "reckless endangerment," which is a serious crime.

Beyond the STD issue, the situation is more blurry. The current understanding of "consent" suggests that when people agree to sexual activity, they do so under certain terms; removing the condom could constitute a violation of those terms, which would theoretically make the sex **nonconsensual**. But it's not clear that this could be successfully prosecuted in court.

However, men who might be tempted to "stealth" someone should be aware that the legal winds are blowing against them. In 2017 a court in Switzerland convicted a man of rape for removing his condom without his partner's permission. It's plausible that similar cases may find their way to North Amreican courts in the future.

Check out this news report on stealthing.

19

EMOTIONAL ABUSE

Of all the types of abuse, physical abuse is the most clear-cut. If someone hits you, you know it. Emotional abuse lies on the other end of the spectrum — people often don't realize it's happening, at least not initially. Both men and women can be emotionally abused, and both can abuse someone else.

It's important to learn how to recognize what emotional abuse is, for two main reasons. First, emotional abuse is itself extremely damaging. The bruises may not be visible, but they exist (metaphorically speaking): low self-esteem, depression, and increased anxiety are just a few of the potential emotional **repercussions**. What's more, severe emotional distress can actually be manifested in the body, for example in the form of chronic pain with no obvious physical cause. An emotionally abusive partner who's making you miserable may literally be making you sick, too.

The other reason it's vital to recognize emotional abuse is that it's frequently the first step down a road leading to violence. It's rare for physically abusive partners to start with hitting — after all, anybody who hits someone on a first date is unlikely to get a second. Instead, abusive behavior generally begins in much subtler ways and gradually ramps up over time. If you've ever wondered why someone stays with an abusive partner, that's a major factor: the partner didn't start out like that! He or she probably seemed wonderful at the beginning.

That said, the word *seemed* is doing a lot of work in the previous sentence. The signs are often there, if you know what to look for. Examples of emotionally abusive behavior include (but aren't limited to) the following:

- threatening to punish or embarrass you if you don't do what your partner wants

TEEN DATING VIOLENCE

- constantly criticizing you, as though you never do anything right
- denying that something happened when it did (this is called "gaslighting," see page 23 for more)

Emotional abusers will try to dominate your perception of what's real and replace your instincts with their own.

DEALING WITH DATING AND ROMANCE

- frequently interrupting you or speaking on your behalf without permission
- violating your privacy (for instance by checking your text messages without your consent)
- giving the "silent treatment" or withholding affection when you are "in trouble" for some reason
- trying to control how you spend your time and who you spend it with
- blaming you for anything that goes wrong, regardless of whether it was something you could realistically control
- hurting your feelings and then telling you it's your own fault
- responding to even mild criticism by steering the conversation toward something you supposedly did wrong ("but what about…?")
- breaking or losing something that matters to you
- showering you with excessive gifts or attention as a way of "making up" for doing something wrong

Emotional abuse can be very specific to the individuals involved — what is abusive in one situation may not be in another. Consider one of the examples above: "breaking or losing something that matters to you." Let's say you have a framed photo from your last family reunion; in the middle of an argument with your partner, the frame ends up smashed on the floor. Was that an abusive move by your partner, or is he or she just a klutz? Only you can know for sure.

Unfortunately, abusers depend on the idea that you *won't* know for sure. A big part of emotional abuse involves undermining your sense of what's true and what's not. It might seem odd to have "gifts and affection" on the above list of abusive behaviors, but it has to do with the way emotional abuse messes with your sense of reality. Excessive gifts and affection are part of a cycle: the abuser hurts you in some way and then goes over the top in attempting to "make up for it." *Clearly I am a good person* — the abuser's thinking goes — *because look at this amazing gift I gave you! If you're still mad about the other thing after this amazing gift, it's you* who are the bad person, not *me.*

But here's the deal: the way to "make up" for problematic behavior is to (1) apologize sincerely and (2) stop doing the thing that caused the problem. Flowers are not apologies. Gifts are not apologies. In fact, flowers and gifts can cover up the fact that the person is not actually apologizing! This is how emotionally abusive relationships can slowly degrade both your self-confidence and your sense of **self-determination**.

WHAT IS GASLIGHTING?

In the 1944 film *Gaslight*, Ingrid Bergman stars as Paula, the young wife of Gregory (Charles Boyer). Gregory forces Paula to leave her family and friends and move in to his creepy house. Things don't go well for Paula there. Gregory is jealous and possessive, and he accuses Paula of strange behaviors that she can't even remember. The lights in the house flicker on and off, but Gregory says Paula is imagining it. *Spoiler alert:* Years earlier, Gregory had murdered Paula's aunt in a botched jewel heist; now he's deliberately trying to drive Paula insane, so that he can get his hands on the fortune she inherited.

Gaslight is a pretty spot-on (if melodramatic) portrait of an abusive relationship. The film and the play on which it's based gave us the term *gaslighting*, for an especially **pernicious** type of emotional abuse.

Gaslighters manipulate other people by making them mistrust their own experiences. Most of us wouldn't lie about something that can easily be

DEALING WITH DATING AND ROMANCE

> "The Gaslight Effect results from a relationship between two people: a gaslighter, who needs to be right in order to preserve his own sense of self and his sense of having power in the world, and a gaslightee, who allows the gaslighter to define her sense of reality because she idealizes and seeks his approval. . . . [A] gaslighter will take advantage of that vulnerability to make you doubt yourself, over and over again."
>
> – Dr. Robin Stern, *The Gaslight Effect*

proven wrong, so hearing someone state obvious lies with a straight face can make us feel crazy. Gaslighters often say one thing and do another, but if you confront them, they deny it and then blame you for bringing up the subject in the first place.

Blatant lies are a big part of gaslighting, and yet gaslighters frequently accuse others of lying. This has two goals: it helps them establish themselves as the sole arbiter of truth, while also redirecting any suspicion off themselves and onto others. Another common strategy is to accuse you of being mean or ungrateful for questioning anything the gaslighter says. That's just another way gaslighters use guilt to manipulate their partners and other people they know.

This video shows how gaslighting can happen in relationships.

DIGITAL ABUSE

The Internet has changed the world in an uncountable number of ways — many positive, but some not. One negative impact of our constant connectivity is the birth of a new category of abusive behavior, called *digital abuse*.

Digital abuse comes in a few general forms. One problem that can arise between romantic partners is one partner trying to control the digital activity of the other. For example, one partner might insist on viewing the other's messages or demand access to passwords. Such demands are considered abusive because they violate the other person's right to privacy. It's important to remember that your digital "identity" — your texts, your Instagram, your Snapchat, and so on — is and should remain *yours*. It's not your partner's to control any more than your body or mind are. And speaking of your body, pressuring someone for explicit pictures is also abusive, and using those pictures to threaten or humiliate someone later is even worse.

The desire for control can also lead an abusive partner to insist that you respond to texts immediately or suffer a guilt trip, argument, or worse. This can be anxiety-inducing if you end up feeling like you need to be "on call" at all times. Again, this isn't okay — you have the right to turn off your phone if you want to! You also have the right to keep your passwords private and to say no to sexting. (For more on digital rights, see page 62.)

Sexting coercion is the term for forcing people to share sexually explicit messages or texts against their will. In 2015 a study from Indiana University found that as many as 25 percent of teens had been pressured for sexually explicit texts and images. Because sexting is a comparatively new activity, people sometimes get confused about what's okay or not okay; they assume "everybody does it, so it must be fine." Let's be clear: *sexting coercion is not okay*. You do not owe *anyone* intimate pictures or texts, no matter who they are.

DEALING WITH DATING AND ROMANCE

Texting is a key part of most contemporary relationships, which is fine — but if texting is used to try to dominate you or coerce you into sexual activities you're not comfortable with, that's not fine.

Another type of digital abuse is one you've surely heard about — alas, it's likely you've already experienced it: using e-mail and social media to threaten, humiliate, or bully another person. This form of digital abuse, usually called *cyberbullying*, can happen in all types of relationships — between total strangers, casual acquaintances, or romantic partners.

It's not uncommon for people who are angry about being rejected romantically to express their anger on social media or in texts. Sometimes this abusive behavior is temporary — the person calms down, accepts the rejection, and moves on. But other times, the situation gets worse,

HOTLINE HELP

Sponsored by the National Center for Victims of Crime, Victim Connect provides information to people who've been the victims of any type of crime, including stalking or other abuse. Operators can answer questions, explain your rights, and make referrals to others who can help you.

Phone: 855-4-VICTIM (855-484-2846)
Chat: chat.victimconnect.org
Web: http://victimconnect.org

TEEN DATING VIOLENCE

ramping up into a second type of abuse called *stalking*. Stalking involves the uninvited surveillance (either online or in person) of another person. It's a form of harassment intended to frighten and intimidate someone.

Authorities worry a lot about stalking because of how easily it can escalate from something minor like annoying texts to in-person confrontations and even violence. Stalking is a situation where it is much better to err on the side of caution. If you are concerned that a former partner is stalking you, it is very important to take that seriously. Discuss the situation with an adult you trust, and please consider bringing the matter to the authorities.

TEXT-DEPENDENT QUESTIONS

1. What are some examples of abusive behaviors?
2. How many teens experience dating violence?
3. How is dating violence related to shootings?
4. What is gaslighting?
5. What does "sexting coercion" refer to?

RESEARCH PROJECT

Read over the section on emotional abuse. Can you think of a moment when you experienced something akin to what is described there? Write about it – describe what happened, what it felt like, and what you thought about afterwards. Are you satisfied with how you responded? Why or why not? If not, write about how you might react differently in the future.

DEALING WITH DATING AND ROMANCE

WORDS TO UNDERSTAND

contentious: describes a heated controversy

credible: believable

entitlement: the sense that one has the right to something

exonerated: cleared of guilt

intermittent: periodic, not regular

internalize: to take in an idea or belief as your own

LGBTQ: acronym for lesbian, gay, bisexual, transgender, and queer/questioning

mete out: dispense

ostracized: shunned, shut out

remorse: regret

scintilla: a tiny amount

sociopath: someone with a severe mental disorder who lacks empathy or conscience

CHAPTER 2

THE DYNAMICS OF ABUSE

Imagine that your best friend starts calling you "dummy" — not in that joking way that pals sometimes do, but genuinely insulting you. Imagine that the two of you are trying to decide on a movie, and your friend grabs you by the wrist and says you'd better do what he (or she) wants, *or else*. Or imagine that the two of you plan to go to the movies, but at the last minute your parents say no, and your friend blames *you* — if you really cared, your friend says angrily, you'd defy your parents. Imagine your best friend suddenly pushing you to the ground, not by accident but on purpose.

Insults, threats, guilt trips, physical abuse. Would you put up with treatment like that from a friend? Probably not, right? But too often, people do put up with behavior like that from their romantic partners. It's confusing when you think about it: the one person who, in theory, should care about you more than any other . . . *that person* treats you worse than any other. Why does that happen? And why do people accept it?

DEALING WITH DATING AND ROMANCE

WHY DO PEOPLE ABUSE OTHERS?

You may have heard it said that rape is not about sex but about control. Much the same can be said for abusive relationships. Although every relationship is different, what all abusive relationships have in common is inequality. One person wants to have all the power, make all the decisions, and **mete out** the punishments for "misbehavior" (which is generally not misbehavior at all!). The abused person is expected to tolerate all of this, while also managing the bad moods of the abuser.

There are a variety of reasons why people abuse their partners – people are complicated, so there's usually not just one reason. But here are a few typical ones:

- **It's what they know.** People often repeat the things they saw their parents do. If they never had models for healthy relationships, how can they know how to behave? Many abusers do the same things they saw others do because it feels "right," even though it feels bad.
- **Abuse or be abused.** People sometimes abuse their partners because they have been abused themselves. It sounds odd, right? If you know that something feels bad when it's done to you, logic suggests you would avoid doing it to others. Unfortunately, humans aren't always so logical. Some people think the world is divided into abusers and victims. They definitely do not want to be

FIND OUT MORE

Do any of the behaviors described here sound familiar? If you are hurting your partner, it's time to break the cycle of abuse and find a way to stop. You are not doomed to be an abusive partner forever – you can change, if you make a real commitment to do so. Start with resources offered by the National Domestic Abuse Hotline, at www.thehotline.org/help/for-abusive-partners/.

THE DYNAMICS OF ABUSE

We learn most of what we know about relationships from watching our parents. If your parents didn't have a healthy relationship, it may be challenging for you to build one – but it's not impossible.

     victims, so they opt to become abusers. Subconsciously, they believe there is no third option.
- **Bullying for power.** Abuse can be understood as a type of severe bullying, and some abusers act out for the same reasons bullies do. They feel insecure, inadequate, and small, so they push other people around to momentarily make themselves feel bigger and more important. The problem, of course, is that bullying is not the same as genuine strength. Dominating another person never solves the problem for long, so the abuser/bully never truly feels any better.
- **Deflection.** It's strange but true: deep down, bullies and abusers are often the most insecure people you'll ever meet. They turn their fears and anxieties

outward, inflicting that pain on others rather than dealing with it themselves. In a sense, an abuser is (metaphorically) saying, "Here, you deal with my pain because I can't or don't want to." This is an especially dangerous dynamic in straight relationships, because women are often trained to be caregivers. They may therefore feel responsible for "fixing" their abuser. (They are not.)

- **Sexism.** Some abusive behaviors spring from a sense of **entitlement** – in this sense, this is the belief (conscious or unconscious) that men have a right to totally control women and ought to be "the boss" in any situation. That may sound very old-fashioned (and it is!), but many teenage boys still feel pressure to be "tough guys" who are in charge all the time.
- **Mental illness.** Finally, some abusers are experiencing some type of mental disorder. It could be addiction, chronic depression, or a condition called "**intermittent** explosive disorder." Then there are the **sociopaths** – people who have no empathy for others and don't care (or even notice) that they are hurting the people they abuse.

There are two important things to understand here. First, whatever the underlying causes might be, none of it makes abuse acceptable. There is no "reason" so good as to make teen dating violence okay. Second, no partner, no matter how loving or patient, can fix these issues for the other person. Whether it's a bad childhood or deep-seated insecurity or a mental health problem, abusers have to address their own problems before they will be able to create healthy relationships with others.

FACT CHECK!

Myth: *Kids who grow up in abusive homes will inevitably repeat the cycle as adults.*

Fact: No, people are not doomed to become their parents. It may take more focus and effort to build a healthy relationship if you never had that model yourself. But the truth is, all healthy relationships take effort. No matter how great *or* terrible our childhoods might have been, we can all learn, grow, and improve.

THE DYNAMICS OF ABUSE

WHY DO PEOPLE STAY?

Maybe even more vexing than "Why do people abuse?" is the question, "Why do people stay?" And again, there are all kinds of reasons:

- **"I don't know where to go."** A very common reason people stay in abusive relationships is because they are not sure they can get by on their own. If a woman has young children, for instance, she may not feel able to simply walk out when she doesn't know where she'll sleep that night.
- **"I can fix it."** Many people, especially women, but also some men, believe that it's their job to be the caretaker of their romantic relationships. The problem is, abusers sense this and take advantage. Some victims put up with abuse because they get so focused on managing their partner's needs that they neglect their own.
- **"It won't happen again."** Because of all the emotions involved, abusive romantic relationships are incredibly complicated. Some abusers cycle between being extremely kind and extremely unkind; for example, they hit their partners but then return the next day full of **remorse** and promises that it will never happen again. Some experts refer to this part of the abuse cycle as the "honeymoon phase," and it's highly deceptive. There is a temptation to dismiss what happened (after all, we all want to be happy). In the honeymoon phase, people tell themselves, "Well, maybe this time *really* will be the last time." Unfortunately, that is *very rarely* the case.
- **Fear of reprisal.** Remember what we said about the number of women who are killed by their ex's. A woman who wants to leave her abuser but feels afraid for her safety is not being paranoid; that is a very real concern, and it needs to be taken seriously.
- **Fear of criticism.** Many are abusers are super-charming to everyone except their partners. Friends may not be particularly supportive of someone who leaves an abusive relationship, because they have no idea what the abuser

DEALING WITH DATING AND ROMANCE

MAKING A "GO BAG"

If you are living with your abuser, the day may come when you need to leave quickly. A "go bag" contains everything you may need, packed in advance so that you can grab it quickly. Things that might "go" in a "go bag" include:

- Change of clothing
- Documents such as birth certificate, social security card, passport
- Extra medications
- Prepaid cell phone
- Spare keys

Keep the bag somewhere you can get to easily, but also somewhere your abuser will not stumble across it. That could be in your house, the trunk of your car, or even a friend's house.

is really like in private. Particularly for teenagers, this can create a powerful incentive to just "put up with it," rather than risk being **ostracized** by their peers.

- **Fear of revenge.** Sometimes people feel trapped in relationships because their partners know too much about them. For instance, the abuser may have intimate photographs and threaten to show them around. Or maybe an abused person is **LGBTQ** but not out yet; an intimate partner might threaten to expose the person's secret.

- **Staying feels bad but correct.** In much the same way that abusers act the way they do because it's what they're used to, victims of abuse sometimes accept the situation because they think that's how life has to be. It's not that they don't know abuse is bad — they do! But even if it feels terrible, it still feels, at some very deep level, like it's expected or even deserved.

- **Leaving feels impossible.** One very real impact of abuse is the destruction of the victim's self-esteem. If the person you love is constantly criticizing you, blaming you for every problem, and making you feel terrible, that can wear you down. If the abuse has been going on for a while, a victim may **internalize** the idea that he or she *does* deserve it, just like the abuser says. People who are being abused frequently feel depressed or anxious — and both of those mental states make it even harder to make a big life change.

LGBTQ RELATIONSHIPS AND ABUSE

Research suggests that people in the LGBTQ community experience abuse in their romantic relationships even more often than straight people. One Centers for Disease Control and Prevention (CDC) study found that while about 35 percent of straight women had been sexual assaulted, physically injured, or stalked by a partner, the numbers rose to 44 percent among lesbians and 61 percent among bisexual women. About 26 percent of gay men and 37 percent of bisexual men had experienced sexual assault, physical violence, or stalking by a partner, as compared to 29 percent of heterosexual men.

Many of the same underlying dynamics that play out in straight relationships, such as a sense of entitlement or a need to gain control over

GETTING HELP

If you are being abused or are concerned about someone who is, these are some LGBTQ-friendly resources.

LGBT National Help Center
www.glbtnationalhelpcenter.org
1-800-246-PRIDE (7743)
Chat: www.glbthotline.org/chat.html

Network LaRed
1-800-832-1901
TTY: 617-227-4911
English site: http://tnlr.org/en
En Espanol: http://tnlr.org/sp

Trans Lifeline
www.translifeline.org
U.S. hotline: 1-877-565-8860
Canada hotline: 1-877-330-6366

Trevor Project
www.thetrevorproject.org
Hotline: 1-866-488-7386
Text START to 678678
Chat: www.thetrevorproject.org/get-help-now

DEALING WITH DATING AND ROMANCE

another, are also involved in LGBTQ relationships. But there are additional factors to consider, too. LGBTQ relationships often don't receive the same levels of social support – from friends, family, and coworkers, and so on – as straight couples do. That can leave people in such relationships feeling isolated, which not only causes stress in the relationship, but also makes abused people more afraid to leave the relationship. Abused partners may also fear being outed if they end the relationship.

Sometimes people in LGBTQ relationships feel a lot of pressure to look "perfect" to the outside world. Shame also plays a role here: if you're already struggling with feelings of shame about your sexual orientation, the last thing you may want to do is admit that you are being abused as well.

Another obstacle is that anti-domestic violence services don't always seem welcoming to LGBTQ people. Sometimes there is genuine discrimination involved, while other times it's more a matter of perception. But it's understandable that LGBTQ abuse survivors might assume that domestic violence services are only intended for straight women. Even when employees at a particular shelter may be gay-friendly, the stereotype of "a woman's shelter" leaves quite a lot of people out in the cold.

All people, regardless of sexual orientation or gender identity, deserve relationships that are free from abuse. If you are a member of the LGBTQ community and are experiencing abuse, there are people who want to help you. Consult the numbers in the box on this page for more information.

Check out this video for more on abuse in LGBTQ relationships.

THE DYNAMICS OF ABUSE

WHAT IS "HOOKUP CULTURE"?

Discussions of teen dating violence sometimes focus on committed couples, and that makes sense. But it's worth taking a moment to talk about more casual relationships, because they can have abusive features too. The reality is, you don't have to be somebody's boyfriend or girlfriend for abuse to happen.

The expression "hookup culture" describes spontaneous casual encounters, which frequently occur during or after parties or other social events. Emotional attachments are, if not forbidden, certainly discouraged. As the author Lisa Wade points out in her book *American Hookup*, one odd result of hookup culture is the idea of having sex with people you are *not* especially interested in. Wade observes that in the minds of millennials, there is a difference between "careless"

DATING SAFETY TIPS

- Go out with friends rather than alone, and look out for one another.
- Don't give out a lot of personal information when you first meet someone. If the two of you hit it off, there'll be plenty of time later to discuss where you live or what your usual routine looks like.
- If you are drinking alcohol, make sure you know what you are consuming; punch, for instance, is not a great idea, because you don't know what's in it.
- Don't let anyone else give you a drink or hold your drink for you.
- Keep your cell phone charged at all times.
- Make sure you are already set up with a ride app like Lyft or Uber, or that you have the number for a cab or car service programmed into your phone.
- If you leave a party with someone you don't know well, make sure your friends know where you are going.
- If you are uncomfortable in any situation, trust your instincts and leave. Don't worry about hurting someone else's feelings – your safety comes first.

DEALING WITH DATING AND ROMANCE

and "careful" sexual activity. The rules of hookup culture involve, in Wade's words, "performing meaninglessness" — that is, everyone has to act as disinterested as possible. According to her research, "all of the kindnesses that go along with romantic relationships are considered off script once casual sex is on the table."

There is a huge potential for heartbreak in hookup culture, as well as (not incidentally) a huge risk of assault and abuse. Wade argues that the norms of hookup culture help facilitate rape because they encourage people to view partners as "things" that can be used and thrown away, rather than as human beings with feelings.

It's not the job of this book to tell you how to feel about hookup culture. But do give some serious thought to whether sex-without-emotions is truly something you want for yourself. One unnamed female college student told National Public Radio in 2017, "I think girls know when they're being used, and I think it feels bad to be used. But I think the alternative is that nobody wants to use you . . . and that [feels] worse."

If hookup culture isn't for you, you are not alone. Media reports make it sound like "everyone is doing it," but that's not true. According to Wade's research, only about 15 percent of college students describe themselves as really interested in hookup culture, while about 30 percent of students want nothing to do with it at all, and the rest are somewhere in between. So while it may seem like college is all about hooking up, the numbers don't bear that out. In fact, 21st-century college students are having roughly the same amount of sex as their parents' generation did.

A lot of hookups start on the dance floor.

THE DYNAMICS OF ABUSE

KAVANAUGH AND FORD: WHAT DID WE LEARN?

Sexual abuse among teenagers became front-page news in the fall of 2018. A federal judge named Brett Kavanaugh was nominated by President Donald Trump to fill an open seat on the U.S. Supreme Court; in the course of a highly **contentious** confirmation hearing, Kavanaugh was accused of attempted sexual assault in 1982. His accuser, Christine Blasey Ford, testified under oath that during a party in high school, Kavanaugh and his friend had trapped her in a bedroom. Ford alleged that Kavanaugh held her down on the bed and groped her while his friend watched and laughed. During his own testimony, Kavanaugh repeatedly and forcefully denied that any of this had ever occurred. In his opening statement to the Senate Judiciary Committee, he blamed the situation on a coordinated smear campaign by political opponents.

Watching the hearings was an emotional experience for many people. But as painful as the hearings were, none of it prevented Kavanaugh's ascension to the Supreme Court; he was sworn in as an associate justice in early October.

Let's set aside the specifics and look at the situation in a general way that's relevant to the topic of this book. After all, no matter whom you believe in this *particular* case, there's no question that many young people do, indeed, experience similar situations. In that context, there are a few points we can take away from what went on in the hearings, and what the hearings suggest about the dynamics of sexual assault, especially among teens.

PUT YOURSELF IN *HIS* PLACE

Many of Kavanaugh's defenders said that they didn't think Ford was lying, *exactly* – instead, they argued that Ford couldn't be certain that it was

brutal rape of an exotic dancer who was at a party held for their lacrosse team. The three young men maintained their innocence throughout, and indeed they were ultimately **exonerated**. The prosecutor in the case was not only disbarred, but ended up being prosecuted himself, for conspiring to hide evidence. But as far as the young men were concerned, the damage was already done. One said, "I don't think it really will ever be over. No matter what, you can try to move on, but 'rape' will always be associated with my name."

In 2017 the University of Oxford's Centre for Criminology studied people who'd been accused but cleared of sexual abuse. The experience was "an enduring trauma" that brought "high anxiety levels, severe depression, [and] ill health," not to mention serious financial and social problems. The study also quoted an activist group called the Community of the Wrongly Accused, who note that allegations of sexual misconduct "are often their own convictions in the high court of public opinion, because the stigma is so severe."

As sexual assault and abuse is dragged from the shadows, it's vital to hold a few ideas in our minds at the same time. One, *in general*, unreported assaults are a greater problem than false reports, and it is more likely that any given accuser is telling the truth than not. Statistics also tell us that men are more likely to be assaulted themselves than to be falsely accused. At the same time, though, we

Residents of Durham, North Carolina, expressed their anger at the news of a horrific rape at Duke University, but it turned out that the accused students were completely innocent.

must never forget that false accusations do happen, and any *specific* accused person might in fact be innocent. A well-intentioned desire to support survivors is not a reason to throw out the long-standing notion that, in the United States, people are considered innocent until proven guilty.

TEXT-DEPENDENT QUESTIONS

1. What are some of the underlying reasons someone might behave abusively toward their partner?
2. What are some reasons why people may find it difficult to leave an abusive relationship?
3. What factors make abuse in LGBTQ relationships alike or different from straight relationships?
4. What is "himpathy"?
5. Roughly what percentage of sexual assault claims are reported to be false by the FBI?

RESEARCH PROJECT

Find out more about the hearings for Judge Kavanaugh and write an essay that argues for or against his confirmation to the Supreme Court. Do you find Dr. Ford's story credible — why or why not? And even if you do, to what extent do you think accusations like these should figure into whether someone gets a seat on the Supreme Court? Is it still a big deal, or should old accusations not matter?

DEALING WITH DATING AND ROMANCE

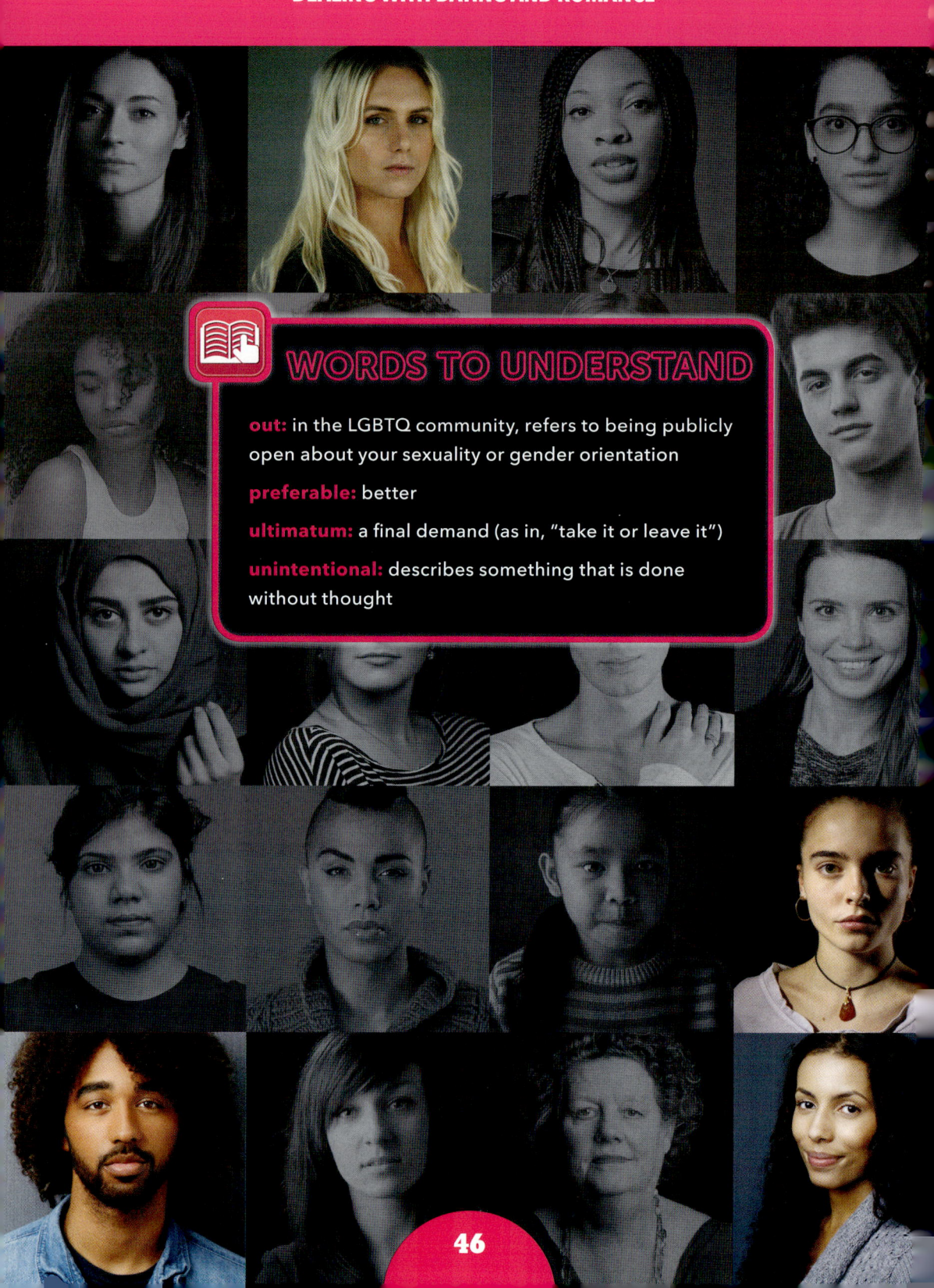

WORDS TO UNDERSTAND

out: in the LGBTQ community, refers to being publicly open about your sexuality or gender orientation

preferable: better

ultimatum: a final demand (as in, "take it or leave it")

unintentional: describes something that is done without thought

46

CHAPTER 3

WHAT DO I DO NOW?

If the abusive behaviors described in this book are happening to you, it's time to do something about it. Don't waste energy criticizing yourself for having "let this happen." You didn't let it happen; it is happening *to* you — and it's not your fault. But there is no bad time to deal with an abusive situation. It's not too late, nor is it too soon.

Maybe the earlier chapters remind you of a friend's relationship. Remember how, earlier in the book, we quoted an estimate that one in three high school students had experienced some type of abuse (physical, sexual, emotional, or a combination). Do you have two or more friends? Statistically speaking, at least one of them either has been or is being abused in some way. Here we'll try to provide practical advice about how you can help a friend who is in an abusive situation.

It's also possible that the actions we've described might remind you not of *other* people's actions, but your own. It could be **unintentional** — you may not have realized the damage that certain behaviors can cause. But now that you're more informed, hopefully you are starting to think about how you can build healthier relationships with the people you care about. This chapter and the next are going to address that, too. It's never too late to do better.

WHAT IS THE RELATIONSHIP SPECTRUM?

Every relationship is different, and only the people in a particular relationship truly know what it's like. What feels right to some people may be totally wrong for others. People have different levels of tolerance for arguing, for instance – some people need to hash everything out frequently, while others are very stressed out by relationships with a lot of conflict. Only you know what is right for you. Listen to what your gut tells you, and don't accept situations or relationships that feel wrong.

The National Dating Abuse Hotline has a super-helpful website called LoveIsRespect.org, and it talks about how relationships exist on a spectrum that goes from healthy to unhealthy to abusive:

- **Healthy relationships** feature good communication; mutual respect and trust; honesty; making decisions as a team; a willingness to compromise; and acceptance of occasional time apart when needed.
- **Unhealthy relationships** are marked by poor communication, which could be fighting or no talking at all; disrespect; a lack of trust and dishonesty; inequality in making decisions; and an unwillingness to have any time apart.
- **Abusive relationships** feature hurtful or demeaning forms of communication; active disrespect for feelings, decisions, and individual choices; emotional cruelty; constantly placing blame and guilt on the partner; and pressuring or forcing the partner to do things they don't want to do.

LoveIsRespect.org has a quiz that you can take to test your knowledge of healthy, unhealthy, and abusive behaviors. Point your browser here: www.loveisrespect.org/dating-basics/relationship-spectrum.

WHAT DO I DO NOW?

BAD SIGNS

When you're in the middle of a relationship, it can be tough to figure out whether a particular incident is just part of a bad day or if it's a sign of worse to come. What follows are some warning signs that ought to make you concerned, whether it's your own relationship or that of a friend. It may be time to worry if someone:

- insults and demeans their partner in public;
- demands control over how their partner spends free time and with whom;
- reacts to minor disagreements with insults, cruelty, or guilt trips;
- refuses to take any responsibility for problems, placing all blame on the partner; and
- makes threats or **ultimatums**.

Those are all pretty obvious red flags, but abuse doesn't always happen in an obvious way. In fact, it's not unusual for a couple to seem perfectly content to others even while things are ugly in private. So here are some other signs to be aware of that might point to hidden abuse. There may be reasons for concern if a friend:

- has bruises or marks that they can't explain or won't talk about;
- abruptly stops interacting with friends and family;
- seems nervous and overly concerned about upsetting their partner;
- is frequently defensive about their partner's behavior;
- seems depressed, anxious, or has other personality changes.

YOU EMBARRASS ME

One way to do a gut-check about the health of your relationship is to ask yourself, "When I talk to my friends, am I honest?"

DEALING WITH DATING AND ROMANCE

Let's say you tell your best friend about the last fight you had with your partner. (Note: you don't have to actually do this, although it might be an interesting experiment. For now, just picture this situation.) What parts of the fight would you share easily, and what parts would you be tempted to hold back? Did your partner say or do anything that you wouldn't want a friend to know about? Did *you* say or do anything you wouldn't want to confess? Deep down, most of us know the difference between right and wrong, and we usually know when we crossed the line.

Now set aside the example of an argument, and just think about what you tell your friends about your partner in general. Are you honest with your friends, and do they like your partner anyway? Or do you feel that you have to lie to your friends about your relationship, just to keep the peace? If you don't feel like you can be totally honest with your friends about the person you're dating, that's a red flag that something may not be right. (A big exception to this is if you are in a LGBTQ relationship but you are not **out**. It's often **preferable** to be out, but not everyone is in a situation where they can do so safely — especially teenagers. If that's the reason you aren't able to be honest about your partner, that's very different from hiding your partner's bad behavior or cruelty.)

How do you portray your relationship when you talk to your friends? Are you more or less honest? Or do you leave details out because you are worried your friends will judge you? That could be a sign that you know, deep down, that something isn't right.

WHAT DO I DO NOW?

GETTING OUT

One of the most difficult aspects of abusive relationships is the fact that, as time goes on, it gets harder to leave, rather than easier.

People who are being abused experience massive damage to their self-esteem. The longer the abuse goes on, the more likely it is for people to believe they deserve it. They do not. *You* do not. Especially if you witnessed or experienced abuse when you were younger, it's easy to assume that such treatment is normal. **It is not normal.** A person who loves you should not be mistreating you, hurting you, or making you feel bad about yourself. No matter who you are, no matter your age, gender, sexual identity, or any other factor, you have a right to healthy relationships that are free from abuse.

Another tricky aspect of abusive relationships is that, as we've noted before, they don't start out abusive, at least not in an obvious way. You need to

CAN MY PARTNER CHANGE

Yes, people can change. It takes a lot of work and a whole lot of commitment, but it's possible. All of us make mistakes, and all of us can try to do better the next time.

Here's an important point, though – while people can change if they really try, *you can't change someone else*. Sometimes people who are being abused tell themselves, "If I just do everything right, it will stop." But that's not true. You can't control how others act. You can only control how you react to others.

If you are in a relationship with an abusive person, you will not be able to fix that person or that behavior. Indeed, you should not try to fix anyone – *especially* if you're a teenager. Do not wait around to see if an abusive person will do better. Find a better person instead.

It may not seem this way to you right now, but there are a whole lot of people in the world who are not abusive. You deserve to be happy with one of them.

DEALING WITH DATING AND ROMANCE

understand that abuse generally starts off with minor things but nearly always gets worse. If your partner is insulting you or making demands about checking your phone, don't dismiss that behavior as "not that bad."

Sometimes people stay in abusive relationships because they don't want to admit the truth of what's going on. They may feel deeply embarrassed about the situation and blame themselves for "letting this happen." It's important to understand that feelings of shame are totally normal but also totally misplaced. You are not the one who should feel shame – the abuser should. In fact, it takes a lot of bravery to step forward and speak the truth. You may feel weak right now, but asking for help is actually a sign of great strength.

If you think you are being abused and you want help, the ideal first step is to take the problem to an adult you know and trust. A parent, a relative, a teacher, a coach, a member of the clergy . . . whoever in your life who is a source of support, that's the person you should approach if possible. Unfortunately, that's *not* possible for everybody all the time. In some situations, you may not have a person like that or you may not feel comfortable going to them for some reason. In such cases, it might be easier emotionally for you to go to someone you don't know that well. A school counselor is a potential resource in this situation. There are also numerous chat lines mentioned throughout this book that might be able to assist you.

Find out more about leaving an abusive relationship.

WHAT DO I DO NOW?

HELPING A FRIEND

If you have a friend who you is being abused, you may be wondering if there is anything you can do. It's tough, because you can't live other people's lives for them. It might seem totally obvious that your friend is in a bad situation, but he or she may not see it quite the same way. There might also be some gaslighting going on – your friend might be believe that the situation is his or her own fault. Your friend's self-esteem might be damaged, which makes it harder for people to stick up for themselves. Lecturing someone about their bad relationship isn't going to change anything. Even if you're right, you could just make the person feel worse. But here are some suggestions on ways you might be able to help:

- **Be ready to listen.** Let your friend know that you are around if he or she wants to talk. Don't apply pressure – just make it clear that you care and will be there if you're needed. When that time comes, try to really hear what your friend has to say, without judgement.

- **Don't act like you know better.** Try to avoid issuing instructions like "You should just dump him." You may very well be right – but it won't help. Telling abused persons to "just leave, already" will likely accomplish nothing but make them feel bad about themselves; to them, it's not that simple – if it were, they would have left already. Even worse, talking that way could make an abused person hold on to the abuser more tightly than ever, because it will feel like "them against the world."

- **Stay neutral about the abuser.** This is a tough one! We all love our friends and want to protect them, so it's natural to get angry at whoever hurts them. But if you sound off about what a jerk the partner is, your friend may feel obligated to go on defense. People who are being abused often feel guilty, embarrassed, and even stupid for being with someone who treats them badly. Harping on how terrible the abuser is might feel good to you – and it might be accurate – but it can backfire.

DEALING WITH DATING AND ROMANCE

- **Stay positive about your friend.** Here's the part where you shouldn't be neutral. Instead of making a big deal about the abuser, make a big deal about your friend. Let your friend know that you believe in them, and that you have their back no matter what. Try to elevate their self-esteem if you can. Maybe you can remember a time where your friend was super-strong, or helped you out, or made a smart decision. A person who is being abused tends to feel like every choice they ever made was wrong. Reminding your friend of positive experiences you've shared might help them remember that there is more to life than this one bad moment.

- **Keep up the gentle encouragement.** Ending a relationship is never easy. It may take a while for your friend to conclude he or she needs to get out. Try to be patient and supportive, and always remember that change may not happen overnight. Keep including your friend in social plans that you make — even if he or she isn't able to join you, it's nice for people to know that they are wanted.

- **Make information available.** There are lots of experts, from counselors and teachers to doctors and police officers, who might be able to help your friend. Gather phone numbers for crisis centers, shelters, or other groups in your community. (There are resources provided throughout this book, so this is a good start, but there are likely other resources that are more local to you.) Make this information available to your friend.

Sometimes it's hard to not try and "solve" our friends' problems for them; but often the best thing you can do for a friend in trouble is to just be there, supportive and listening.

WHAT DO I DO NOW?

However, be sure to pass along the information privately and carefully. Depending on the situation, getting caught with the business card of a domestic violence hotline could get an abused person in trouble with the abuser. Talk to your friend about what resources they might need, how you can help get that information, and the safest way to share it.

- **Some secrets are too big to keep.** As a general rule, it's important to keep your friend's confidence and not share what he or she tells you about the relationship. People who are being abused are naturally afraid to trust anyone with that information, so it's key that you be a strong, dependable friend. However, if you have reason to think your friend is in physical danger, find a trustworthy adult and ask for help. Don't try to handle physical threats alone, and if your friend is in danger, don't keep that to yourself.

TEXT-DEPENDENT QUESTIONS

1. What is the relationship spectrum?
2. What are some signs that there may be abuse in a relationship?
3. Can abusive partners change? Should you wait to see if your partner changes?
4. If you are in an abusive relationship, who are some people who might be able to help?
5. How can you help a friend who is struggling to leave an abusive relationship?

RESEARCH PROJECT

Find out about resources for people dealing with abuse in your own community. Is there a shelter? A hotline? What resources does your school offer? Talk to your nurse or guidance counselor about what they recommend, and turn the information into a poster or pamphlet that can be shared to help people in your community.

DEALING WITH DATING AND ROMANCE

WORDS TO UNDERSTAND

align: line up with, agree with

combatants: warriors

gambit: scheme; tactic

productive: useful

volatile: highly changeable; going from one extreme to the other without warning

CHAPTER 4

BUILDING HEALTHY RELATIONSHIPS

This book includes a lot of information about bad behavior — about the types of actions that are abusive and the harm they can do. But what about the positive side? What does a healthy relationship look like, and how do you build one?

One thing to remember is that everybody is different, so what feels "healthy" to some people may not feel that way to everyone. How couples deal with conflict is a good example. Some couples argue frequently and energetically, and that's healthy *for them*. These couples want to get complaints out in the open, rather than holding them back. Some people just need to "have it out" from time to time.

But other couples hate conflict and find arguments — especially energetic ones — to be difficult and even painful. People who fall into this camp need to work out their problems slowly and quietly, with lots of mutual respect and gentleness on both sides.

Neither type of conflict style is good or bad, they're just different. The key is to find someone whose wants and needs **align** with your own. Then the two of you can work together to build a relationship based on honesty, kindness, and mutual respect.

DEALING WITH DATING AND ROMANCE

WHAT IS A HEALTHY RELATIONSHIP?

Although relationships are different, there are a few basic elements that all good ones have in common. Here are the main ones:

- **Honesty.** The rule "don't lie to your partner" seems so obvious it barely needs to be mentioned . . . but it's so key that we should cover it anyway. Seriously, don't lie. And don't pretend to be someone other than who you really are — that's a form of lying, too. You want to be with someone who can love and appreciate the real you, not some "act" that you put on.
- **Trust.** This is always a scary one, because nobody wants to get hurt. So it may feel safer to be suspicious all the time. But without a basic level of trust, any tiny little misunderstanding can blow up into a big problem. Do you want to get into an argument every time you work on a chemistry project with your attractive lab partner because your romantic partner doesn't trust you? No, you do not. Nor do you want to have an anxiety attack every time your romantic partner is a bit slow to respond to a text. You have to trust each other and — this is important — you both have to act in ways that earn the trust of the other person.
- **Communication.** You aren't psychic, right? Well, neither is your partner. So how can you know which actions will reinforce trust and which won't? You talk. Be open

Find out more about boundaries.

BUILDING HEALTHY RELATIONSHIPS

We all deserve kindness, trust, and mutual respect in our relationships.

DEALING WITH DATING AND ROMANCE

about what you need and want. Just as importantly, listen carefully when your partner does the same. Try to avoid assumptions about what's okay or what's not okay in any given situation. Instead, ask.

- **Healthy boundaries.** The term *boundaries* sounds complicated, but it's a really simple idea: it refers to the fact that each person in the relationship is an individual with his or her own ideas, needs, and feelings. People in healthy relationships understand and respect that their partners exist as separate beings who may have different priorities sometimes, and that's okay. People in healthy relationships can be apart for short periods — to see friends and family, pursue school or work opportunities, or other reasons — and then feel happy to be reunited, rather than being scared or resentful. The fact that you are both unique individuals is a *good* thing to be celebrated, not a bad thing to be worried about or papered over with "little white lies."

- **Kindness.** It's amazing how often we overlook the simple need to be nice to the people we're dating. Somehow, demonstrations of kindness become things we save for people we don't know well, rather than directing some of that loving energy toward the people who are closest to us.

FACT CHECK!

Myth: *If you had a friend who was abusing his partner, you would definitely know.*

Truth: There are a small number of abusers who are total monsters and everybody around them knows it. But abuse situations are rarely that simple. In fact, precisely what makes abusive relationships so difficult is that abusers are just people like anybody else. They can be nice sometimes — even genuinely loving. Some abusers are great friends to other people while treating their partners terribly. That makes the situation very confusing for the person being abused. People on the outside look at the relationship and think, "No, he can't be an abuser, he's such a great guy!"

BUILDING HEALTHY RELATIONSHIPS

Relationship Bill of Rights

You have rights in your relationship. Everyone does, and those rights can help you set boundaries that should be respected by both partners in a healthy relationship.

- You have the right to privacy, both online and off
- You have the right to feel safe and respected
- You have the right to decide who you want to date or not date
- You have the right to say no at any time (to sex, to drugs or alcohol, to a relationship), even if you've said yes before
- You have the right to hang out with your friends and family and do things you enjoy, without your partner getting jealous or controlling
- You have the right to end a relationship that isn't right or healthy for you
- You have the right to live free from violence and abuse

– From LoveIsRespect.org, "Healthy Relationship: High School Educators Toolkit, www.loveisrespect.org/wp-content/uploads/2016/08/highschool-educators-toolkit.pdf

TAKE THE DATING PLEDGE

"I, (name), promise myself, future and current partners to maintain relationships that are based on respect, equality, trust and honest communication. I will value my partner's boundaries online and behind closed doors. I will never engage in any type of abuse – physical, emotional, sexual, financial or digital.

If one of my friends experiences abuse, I pledge to help them by saying something, modeling healthy communication and connecting them to resources.

I pledge to remember, demonstrate and promote the fact that love is respect."

– From LoveIsRespect.org, "Take the Dating Pledge," www.loveisrespect.org/resources/other-campaigns/take-actiontake-the-dating-pledge/

DIGITAL HEALTH

Social media and texting play huge roles in the way we interact with one another, and especially in the ways we date. The National Domestic Violence Hotline recommends that people in new relationships create a "digital contract" that outlines what is acceptable behavior and what is not. It doesn't need to literally be written down – though it certainly could be, if you want! But the "contract" doesn't need to be that formal.

What you do need is an honest discussion about how you and your partner like to use social media and texting, and to what extent you'll incorporate digital technology into your relationship. There are important questions the two of you should discuss, so that both of you are clear on what the other person likes and dislikes, such as:

- Is it okay to talk about your relationship on social media? What's acceptable to share and what's TMI?
- Is it okay to tag the other one? When might it not be okay?
- Is checking in via text okay? How much is too much?
- What do you both think is a reasonable amount of time to respond to a text?
- What's your level of comfort with intimate texts or images? (While considering that question, keep in mind that texting is not 100 percent secure. Once you send that flirty image or comment, you can't completely control what happens to it. Not now and not months later, even after you may have split from this person.)

FIND OUT MORE

See what else the National Domestic Abuse Hotline has to say about digital rights. Point your browser to www.thehotline.org/2014/03/18/what-is-digital-abuse/.

BUILDING HEALTHY RELATIONSHIPS

DATING APPS

If you're still in high school, your dating "prospects" are probably still limited to people in your community. But as you get older, you may choose to interact with people on one of the many dating apps that have proliferated over the last few years. Dating apps can be great, but it's important to be aware of safety issues. After all, you never really know who you're talking with until you meet in person. That can be exciting but also risky. Here are some basic safety tips about dating online:

- Don't offer lots of personal information upfront. There will be plenty of time to share that stuff once you have gotten to know who the person really is.

- Online search tools are your friends. There's nothing wrong with looking up the person to see if what you're being told is true.

- If you plan to meet in person, make sure the first meeting is held in a public place. Tell a trusted friend where you are going and when you expect to return.

DEALING WITH DATING AND ROMANCE

- Is it okay for you to use one another's phones, or no?
- How do you feel about following each other's friends, for example on Instagram? Okay or not okay? What about commenting on friends' posts? Everybody has different answers to these questions, and that's fine — there's no "right" or "wrong" here. What's important is that you and your partner have an open discussion about digital boundaries. Understanding your partner's thoughts and feelings about this issue up front may save you a lot of heartache later.

Most of us spend a lot of time interacting with other people on phones, tablets, or other devices. It's easy to think of those interactions as somehow "less real" than interactions that happen face-to-face. But of course that's not true. Safety and mutual respect are just as important online as they are anywhere else.

BUILDING HEALTHY RELATIONSHIPS

HAS THIS HAPPENED TO YOU?

Here are some situations that may test you in your new relationship, followed by some things you should consider in your response.

You catch your partner reading the texts on your phone. When you ask why, they say they're just curious about what's going on in your life.
Good boundaries include technological boundaries — if your partner wants to know about what's going on in your life, they should ask you directly. Your partner shouldn't be sneaky, try to force you to share, or make you feel guilty about wanting to keep your phone and passwords private.

Your parents announce that you need to stay home this weekend for some "family time." Your partner gets mad and says if you really cared about your relationship, you'd skip family time.
This doesn't rise to the level of abuse, but it's not healthy behavior, either. The partner in this scenario is being overly controlling. You have the right to spend time with your family without being guilt-tripped or pressured about it. Perhaps your partner is feeling insecure in the relationship; if so, that's something the two of you should address together, without dragging your family time into it.

You like kissing your partner but don't feel ready to go any farther than that. Your partner doesn't try to force you, but they do sulk and say that if you really loved them, you would.
Unfortunately this is a common scenario with teens, and it's not okay at all. In a healthy relationship, while one partner might feel somewhat disappointed, that should never turn into pressure or guilt trips. If your partner puts such a high priority on sexual activity that they make you feel bad about going at your

DEALING WITH DATING AND ROMANCE

own pace, then this is not the right partner for you.

You and your partner's best friend are in the same math class. Sometimes you and the friend text each other to get help on particularly hard homework. When your partner finds out, they go ballistic with jealousy. Later, they apologize but say, "it's just because I love you."

> **FACT CHECK!**
>
> **Myth:** Once guys start sexual activity, they are not able to stop.
>
> **Fact:** That's nonsense. If a guy is being intimate with someone and his mom walks in, do you think he keeps going and says, "Sorry, Mom, but I can't stop?" No, of course not. Don't fall for this **gambit**.

Jealousy is understandable, but that doesn't make it healthy. It's true that being in love can make you feel vulnerable and easily spooked — that's natural. But a healthy response to those feelings is to talk to your partner about feeling insecure. Bottling up those feelings and then freaking out when your partner talks to someone else is an unhealthy response. Jealousy is *not* a demonstration of love.

Your partner is super moody a lot of the time. One minute everything will be good, but then you'll say the wrong thing and they will be totally furious — yelling at you, insulting you, telling you everything is your fault, and so on. But then the next day, your partner is super, extra nice to make up for it.

Everybody has a bad day now and again, and we've all said stuff we regretted later. But if your partner is highly **volatile**, constantly yo-yo-ing from happy to angry or scary, that's not a good sign. You are not responsible for managing somebody else's moods. What's more, being super-extra-nice doesn't "fix" having been mean earlier. What fixes having been mean is (a) a sincere apology and (b) taking steps to not be so mean in the future!

BUILDING HEALTHY RELATIONSHIPS

CONFLICT 101

Relationships can be tough. On the one hand, you want to protect yourself and make sure you don't get hurt or taken advantage of. On the other hand, you want to be good to your partner and not hurt him or her. Balancing these two instincts can be very tricky. Even people who've been married for decades still need to hash things out from time to time.

But while *getting* mad comes pretty naturally to most of us, arguing with a partner is a skill that needs to be learned. There are good and bad ways to argue. Here are some tips on handling conflict in a **productive** way:

Keep calm and step away: When a conflict first arises, you may be too upset in the moment to discuss it productively. Maybe you feel hurt by something your

It's okay if you need to take a little break from an argument and gather your thoughts.

DEALING WITH DATING AND ROMANCE

partner said, or angry about something that happened. The desire to lash out is totally understandable, but it's not helpful and you should resist it if you can. Give yourself a moment to calm down, then come back to talk about what happened.

. . . But do come back to talk: When you're trying to work through a problem with your partner, do it in person. Texting, phone calls, and e-mails aren't great for emotional conversations for a few reasons. For one thing, you can't see the other person's reaction to what you are saying; you'll only *truly* know that you've made yourself clear when you can see the other person's face. Talking face to face means that if you *haven't* made yourself clear, you will realize it

An argument with your partner isn't a legal filing — don't try to "win" it. Instead, try to make yourself understood and to understand where the other person is coming from.

BUILDING HEALTHY RELATIONSHIPS

ARGUMENT EXCEPTION

The advice about always having relationship discussions in person does *not* apply to a partner who might hurt you physically. If you have reason to worry that a conversation could turn violent, *you are not responsible for having that conversation in person.*

If that sounds like your situation, please contact an adult you trust for help. It could be a parent or relative, a teacher or coach, a church leader, or even the police . . . anyone you trust to help you. If there's no one available who fits that description, try the LoveIsRespect.org dating violence hotline:

Chat at www.loveisrespect.org
Text LOVEIS to 22522
Call 1-866-331-9474

quickly and can correct it. A misunderstood text can make your partner upset about something you didn't even intend! Things then get worse because you never had a chance to say "no no, that's not what I meant."

In addition, people tend to be gentler with one another in person; we've all had the experience of typing something that we'd never say to someone's face. Difficult discussions have a better chance of resolving, rather than escalating, when people are in the same room.

Winning is actually *not* the thing: The ultimate goal of a romantic argument is to get a problem out into the open and figure out how to solve it. The goal is *not* to "win" by proving that you are right and the other person is wrong. You and your partner are not lawyers tasked with convicting one another. And you don't get any extra points for sarcastic comments or withering insults. Again, it's very human to momentarily want the other person to feel as bad as you do, but it's not going to get you anywhere, and in fact will make the situation worse. Try to focus your energy on truly hearing and understanding what the other person is saying, rather than thinking up a good comeback.

DEALING WITH DATING AND ROMANCE

FIND OUT MORE

Saying "sorry" is important, but it's not enough to just say the word. You have to make a conscious effort to avoid repeating whatever you had to apologize for. These sites have some thoughts on apologies that are worth checking out:

- "What Makes a Good Apology": http://trailheadcounseling.com/makes-good-apology
- "How to Apologize Properly": https://verilymag.com/2014/08/how-to-apologize-properly
- "When 'Sorry' Isn't Enough": www.thehotline.org/2018/07/11/when-sorry-isnt-enough

But what about . . . : When we argue with our partners about one situation, we're often tempted to bring in other, unrelated issues. One partner says, "I don't like it when you do X," and the other says, "Well, what about when *you* do Y?" This is unhelpful, because X and Y are different. Both complaints may be completely legitimate, of course. But complaint Y doesn't *erase* complaint X, or vice versa — they're separate issues. Try to work through X and then move to Y as a different topic.

What I like about you: When you're angry with your partner, you're focused on their worst qualities. That's to be expected, because you're mad! But when you sit down to work out your problems, try to remember that there are (or were!) reasons why you began dating this person. Try to remember *that* version of your partner — the one you care about, the one who cares about you. If partners approach each other as enemy **combatants**, things won't get any better.

Sometimes things end: Ultimately, the goal of an argument is to work through whatever it is that's making you upset and get back to the part that makes you

BUILDING HEALTHY RELATIONSHIPS

happy. Unfortunately, that's not always possible. Sometimes you can't get back to the good part. Relationships come in all shapes, sizes, and life spans; maybe this one has run its course. That doesn't mean you are a failure; it just means this relationship isn't right for you anymore. Likewise, if your partner wants to end things, you *must* accept that he or she has the right to do so.

You probably don't want to hear this from a book, but it really is okay. In all likelihood you'll fall in love with a whole bunch of people in the course of your life. Maybe you and your ex will become good friends one day, or maybe you won't. In either case, you will be okay.

TEXT-DEPENDENT QUESTIONS

1. What are some of the important parts of a healthy relationship?
2. What are boundaries?
3. What are some of your digital rights?
4. If someone is mean to you but gives you a present later, does that fix matters? What would?
5. What are some tips for arguing more productively?

RESEARCH PROJECT

Using this book and additional resources you find on your own, create a list of ways you can work to build healthier romantic relationships. Turn the information into a pamphlet or poster that can be shared

SERIES GLOSSARY OF KEY TERMS

adjudicated: when a problem is addressed in a formal setting, such as a courtroom

advocacy: championing or arguing for a particular thing

agency: the ability to take actions that affect your life or the world

allegations: claims that someone has done something wrong

amorphous: something with a vaguely defined shape

assess: evaluate

cisgender: describes a person whose gender identity matches that person's biological sex

coercion: forcing someone to do something they don't want to do

cognitive: relates to how a person thinks

complainant: legal term for someone who brings a case against another person

conflict resolution: a process through which people with disagreements can work together to solve them

consent: agreement or permission

corroborating: something that confirms a claim is true

credible: believable

demographic: relates to the different types of people in a society; age, race, and gender are examples of demographic categories

deterrent: something that discourages a particular activity

diagnosable: a health condition with specific symptoms and treatments that can be identified by a health-care professional

disordered: random; without a system

dissonance: a tension caused by two things that don't fit together

emancipated: free from certain legal or social restrictions

endemic: widespread or common among a certain group

entitlement: the sense that one has the right to something

exonerated: cleared of guilt

feign: to pretend to feel something you don't

felony: a category of serious crime; felony crimes come in several degrees, with "first degree" being the most serious, "second degree" being slightly less serious, and so on

fondling: to stroke or caress, usually with a sexual implication

idealized: describes something viewed as perfect, or better than it is in reality

incapacitated: describes the condition of being unable to respond, move, or understand

inflection point: a term borrowed from mathematics; refers to moments when

SERIES GLOSSARY OF KEY TERMS

there is a noticeable change (for example in public opinion)

ingratiate: to actively try to get someone to like you

internalize: to take in an idea or belief as your own

intrusive: describes something unwanted, such as "intrusive thoughts"

involuntary: a situation where you have no choice

LGBTQ: acronym for lesbian, gay, bisexual, transgender, and queer/questioning

mandatory: legally required

minor: anyone under the age of legal responsibility; usually means under 18 years old

nonconsensual: describes an act (often sexual) that one participant did not agree to

nontraditional: different from a widely accepted norm

norms: standards of what's considered typical or "normal" for a particular group or situation

nuanced: describes something that is complex; not "black and white"

nurturing: describes something that is supportive and warm

ostracized: shunned, shut out

pernicious: describes something that's very harmful but in a subtle way

pervasive: widespread

prophylactic: preventative

psychosis: mental impairment so severe the person loses connection with reality

PTSD: an acronym for post-traumatic stress disorder, a serious psychological condition caused by profoundly disturbing experiences

regressive: moving backwards, toward an earlier state of being

remorse: regret

repercussions: consequences

resilience: the ability to recover from difficulties

retaliation: revenge or punishment

self-determination: the ability to make your own decisions and follow through with them

sociopath: someone with a severe mental disorder who lacks empathy or conscience

spectrum: a range

STDs: acronym for sexually transmitted diseases

stereotype: a widely held but oversimplified or inaccurate picture of a particular type of person or group

suggestive: describes something that suggests or implies a particular idea

surveillance: observation; spying

trafficking: describes some form of illegal trade or commerce

unambiguous: very clear; not open to interpretation

FURTHER READING & INTERNET RESOURCES

BOOKS AND ARTICLES

Domitrz, Michael. *Can I Kiss You?: A Thought-Provoking Look at Relationships, Intimacy, and Sexual Assault.* Greenfield, WI: Awareness Publications, 2016.

Edwards, Stassa. "Philosopher Kate Manne on 'Himpathy,' Donald Trump, and Rethinking the Logic of Misogyny." Jezebel.com, February 8, 2018. https://jezebel.com/philosopher-kate-manne-on-himpathy-donald-trump-and-r-1822639677.

Feuereisen, Patti. "Some Teen Girls Never Tell." *Ms.* Magazine blog, September 24, 2018. http://msmagazine.com/blog/2018/09/24/teen-girls-never-tell.

Freitas, Donna. *Consent on Campus: A Manifesto.* New York: Oxford University Press, 2018.

Gay, Roxane, ed. *Not That Bad: Dispatches from Rape Culture.* New York: Harper Perennial, 2018.

Hemmen, Lucie. *The Teen Girl's Survival Guide: 10 Tips for Making Friends, Avoiding Drama, and Coping with Social Stress.* Oakland, CA: New Harbinger, 2015.

Langford, Jo. *The Pride Guide: A Guide to Sexual and Social Health for LGBTQ Youth.* Lanham, MD: Rowman & Littlefield, 2018.

Messinger, Adam M. *LGBTQ Intimate Partner Violence: Lessons for Policy, Practice, and Research.* Berkeley: University of California Press, 2017.

Murray, Jill. *But He Never Hit Me: The Devastating Cost of Non-Physical Abuse to Girls and Women.* Lincoln, NE: iUniverse, 2007.

Stern, Robin. *The Gaslight Effect: How to Spot and Survive the Hidden Manipulation Others Use to Control Your Life.* 2007. Foreword by Naomi Wolf. 2nd ed. New York: Harmony Books, 2018.

Wade, Lisa. *American Hookup: The New Culture of Sex on Campus.* New York: W.W. Norton, 2017.

FURTHER READING & INTERNET RESOURCES

WEBSITES

Love Is Respect.
> https://www.loveisrespect.org
>
> A project of the National Domestic Violence Hotline, this is a thorough, supportive, and helpful website about teen dating violence and how to build healthier relationships. Includes access to a 24/7 chat line. Highly recommended.

Safe Dates: An Evidence-Based Program to Prevent Dating Violence.
> https://www.hazelden.org/web/go/safedates
>
> An educational program to prevent dating violence from the Hazelden Betty Ford Foundation.

The Trevor Project.
> https://www.thetrevorproject.org
>
> Crisis intervention and resources for LGBTQ youth.

Youth.gov. "Dating Violence Prevention."
> https://youth.gov/youth-topics/teen-dating-violence
>
> Lots of information on teen dating violence and how to combat it; from the U.S. government and the CDC.

EDUCATIONAL VIDEOS

Chapter 1

Check out this news report on stealthing.
> http://x-qr.net/1Ldc

This video shows how gaslighting can happen in relationships.
> http://x-qr.net/1HvH

Chapter 2

Check out this video for more on abuse in LGBTQ relationships.
> http://x-qr.net/1J0K

Chapter 3

Find out more about leaving an abusive relationship.
> http://x-qr.net/1KSn

Chapter 4

Find out more about boundaries.
> http://x-qr.net/1J2b

INDEX

A

abuse, reasons why
    abuse or be abused, 30
    bullying for power, 31
    deflection, 31–32
    mental illness, 32
    sexism, 32
    sociopaths, 32
    what they know, 30
abusive behaviors
    behavior of victims, 33–34
    blaming the victim, 47
    dating and, 8–9
    digital abuse, 25–27, 62–65
    emotional abuse, 20–24
    escaping abusive relationship, 51–52
    false accusations of, 39–41, 43–45
    LGBTQ relationships, 35–36
    physical violence, 16
    reasons why, 30–32
    rough sex play, 18
    sexual abuse, 17–19, 42
    signs of abuse, 49–50, 65–66
    warning signs of, 12
American Psychological Association, 14
Archibald, Andrea Bastiani, 42
assault, 16

B

battery, 16
bullying, 26, 31

C

Centers for Disease Control and Prevention (CDC)
    demographics of abuse victims, 35
    male victims of sexual assault, 43
    rate of physical violence in America, 16
    survey of students, 8–9
coercion, 10, 18
Community of the Wrongly Accused, 44
contentious, 28
correlation, 10, 15
credible, 28, 41
cyberbullying, 26

D

dating, 8–9
dating apps, 63
dating pledge, 61
dating safety tips, 37
digital abuse
    cyberbullying, 26
    digital contract, 62, 64

INDEX

explicit pictures, 25
setting boundaries, 65
sexting, 25
sexting coercion, 25
stalking, 27
violating privacy, 25
domestic violence. *see also* teen dating violence
    behavior of victims, 33–34
    connection to mass shootings, 14–15
    cost of, 16
    escaping abusive relationship, 51–52
    murder rate of women, 14
Duke University lacrosse players, 43–44

E

emotional abuse
    blame, 22
    breaking or losing others' possessions, 22
    constant criticism, 21
    controlling behavior, 22
    excessive gifts or attention, 22–23
    frequently interrupting, 22
    gaslighting, 21, 23–24
    hurting others' feelings, 22
    threats to punish or embarrass, 20
    violating privacy, 22
    withholding affection, 22

entitlement, 28
exonerated, 28, 44

F

false accusations of sexual abuse, 39–41, 43–45
Ford, Christine Blasey, 39–41

G

Gaslight, movie, 23
gaslighting, 21, 23–24
gift giving, 22–23
Girl Scouts, 42
Great Mills High School shootings, 14

H

hookup culture, 8, 37–38

I

intermittent, 28
internalize, 28, 34
intimate partner violence. *see* teen dating violence

K

Kavanaugh, Brett, 39–41
Kennedy, Senator John, 41

L

LGBT National Help Center, 35

LGBTQ relationships, 28, 34, 35–36, 50

M

Manne, Kate, 41

Marjory Stoneman Douglas School shootings, 14

mass shootings, 14–15

mental illness, 32

mete out, 28

N

National Center for Victims of Crime, 26

National Dating Abuse Hotline, 48

National Domestic Abuse Hotline, 30, 62

National Domestic Violence Hotline, 9

Network LaRed, 35

nonconsensual, 10

nontraditional, 10, 11

O

ostracized, 28, 34

out, 46, 50

P

pernicious, 10, 23

physical violence, 16

preferable, 46, 50

R

rape, 17

reckless endangerment, 19

relationships
- bill of rights, 61
- conflict in, 67–71
- healthy, 58–61
- how to help a friend, 53–55
- signs of abuse, 12, 49–50, 65–66
- social media, 62–65
- spectrum of, 48

remorse, 28

repercussions, 10

S

Santa Fe High School shootings, 14

scintilla, 28, 41

self-determination, 10, 23

sexism, 32

sexting, 25

sexual abuse, 17–19, 39–41, 42, 43–45

sexually transmitted disease, 19

social media, 25–27, 62–65

sociopaths, 28, 32

spectrum, 10, 12

stalking, 27

statutory rape, 17

stealthing, 18–19

INDEX

T

teen dating violence
- abusive behaviors, 12
- boy will be boys, 42
- digital abuse, 25-27
- domestic violence, 12
- emotional abuse, 20-24
- escaping abusive relationship, 51-52
- hookup culture, 37-38
- how to help a friend, 53-55
- mass shootings and, 14-15
- physical violence, 16
- scope of, 14-15
- sexual abuse, 17-19
- signs of abuse, 49-50, 65-66
- stealthing, 18-19

Trans Lifeline, 35

Trevor Project, 35

U

ultimatum, 46, 49

unambiguous, 10, 18

unintentional, 46, 47

University of Oxford Centre for Criminology, 44

V

victims of abuse
- behavior of, 33-34
- escaping abusive relationship, 51-52
- go bag, 34
- how to help a friend, 53-55

W

Weiss, Bari, 41

women, murder rate of, 14

AUTHOR'S BIOGRAPHY

H.W. Poole is a writer of books for young people, including *The Big World of Fun Facts* (Lonely Planet Kids) and the sets *Childhood Fears and Anxieties*, *Families Today*, and *Mental Illnesses and Disorders* (Mason Crest). She created the *Horrors of History* series (Charlesbridge) and the Ecosystems series (Facts On File). She was coauthor and editor of *The History of the Internet* (ABC-CLIO), which won the 2000 American Library Association RUSA award.

PHOTO CREDITS

Note: Individuals pictured are models and are used for illustrative purposes only.
Portraits on cover and throughout interior: Shutterstock: AlohaHawaii (54776611); Armin Staudt (562438669); ESP Professional (139687573); Jaruwan Jaiyangyuen (543452206); paffy (190924796); PicMy (1109985788); pio3 (556184392); Ranta Images (1010065381); Ranta Images (1088056442); Roberts Photography (370552535); Rudo film (1021189897); sasha2109 (1036424044); Sergey Mironov (187893986); Stock-Asso (442006258); stockfour (198421241); stockfour (359877911); stockfour (392891674); VladOrlov (532325506); wavebreakmedia (643257913); wavebreakmedia (643261894).
Dreamstime: 13 top, Godfer (17342785); 13 bottom, Rawpixelimages (97129162); 13 left ID Karelnoppe (75833164); 18 Andriy Petrenko (30299595); 21 Tommaso79 (73046697); 26 Antonio Guillem (126968892); 31 Eakachai Leesin (66341197); 38 Mirko Vitali (94183126); 40 Karl Sonnenberg (127857219); 42 Iakov Filimonov (95273340); 50 Dtiberio (84134880); 54 Antonio Guillem (96415230); 59 Irene (87479877); 63 Antonio Guillem (66845433); 64 Saša Prudkov (36864999); 67 Ian Allenden (62933525); 68 Scott Griessel (26777055).
Wikimedia: 15 Voice of America; 44 KWSutton